CONTENTS

A special thank you to Lewisham shopping, who made it possible for 6,000 children in the borough to receive this book free of charge. If you bought a copy, £1 will be donated to Demelza Hospice Care for Children (www.demelza.org.uk).

This book is dedicated to my parents, Jean & Ken Barr MBE, in gratitude for the sacrifices they made to give me a great education in South East London.

INTRODUCTION

When I first set out to write this book, I didn't think I would find much to write about Lewisham's history. As it turned out, there's so much that the biggest challenge was deciding what to leave out!

I've concentrated on people and subjects that I think will be of interest to younger members of the family (though I'm sure adults will enjoy reading about them too). There's information on every town in the borough, as well as wider historical topics. You might not want to read every single chapter, but I hope you enjoy finding out more about where you live, work or go to school.

Looking at Lewisham* today, it's hard to imagine that only 200 years ago it was mostly fields, woods and quaint villages. 'Leafy Lewisham', as it was known, was not even in London then – it was part of Kent. But, as you will see, it has an amazing story to tell!

* The London Borough of Lewisham, including Bellingham, Brockley, Catford, Downham, Forest Hill, Grove Park , Hatcham , Hither Green, Ladywell, Lee, Lewisham, New Cross, Southend and Sydenham, as well as parts of Blackheath, Deptford and Honor Oak.

RAIDERS & SETTLERS

People have been living in what we now know as the London Borough of Lewisham since the Stone Age, hundreds of thousands of years ago.

Much of the area then was covered with dense forests, which provided a plentiful supply of wood for building, burning and boat-making. Being close to an endless supply of clean, fresh water made a lot of sense too; that's why the earliest settlements were often located near rivers, and preferably ones with relatively shallow water, so they could be crossed easily. In Lewisham's

▼ A typical Iron Age settlement

case, it would have been the River Ravensbourne and its tributaries, the Pool and Quaggy, which flow into the River Thames at Deptford Creek.

These early Britons did not write down their history, so archaeologists have had to reconstruct it as best they can from evidence found buried in the ground... and by using their imaginations!

Fortunately, the Roman General Julius Caesar, who launched unsuccessful invasions of Kent in 55BC and 54BC, kept detailed records of his many expeditions and battles. He once wrote a description of the local Kent tribespeople, who must have looked pretty scary: 'All the Britons dye their body with woad, which produces a blue colour and gives them a wild appearance. They wear their hair long; every other part of the body except the upper lip they shave'.

Although they were always arguing and fighting with neighbouring tribes, the ancient Britons were actually quite a cultured people. Archaeologists have unearthed ornate jewellery, gold, silver, bronze and tin coins and evidence that they were expert potters and weavers.

In 43AD the Roman General Aulus Plautius landed on the Kent coast at Rutupiae (Richborough) under strict orders from

▶ A street scene in second century Roman Britain

Emperor Claudius to conquer Britain once and for all. The Britons again put up a brave fight, but this time the invasion force of more than 40,000 soldiers triumphed. After a series of bloody battles over many years, Britain – like most of Europe –became a Roman colony. Roman burials, buildings and other artefacts found in the borough are reminders of its strategic location on Watling Street. This Roman road, which we now call the A2, linked the important town of Londinium (London) to the port of Dubris (Dover).

From the third century onwards, raiders from continental Europe began attacking Kent. Other parts of the Roman empire were also being targeted. Finally, in the early part of the fifth century, Roman soldiers were ordered to leave Britain for good. Some of the newcomers decided to set up home here. First came tribes of Saxons from North Germany and Holland and Angles and Jutes from Denmark. We use one name to describe all these groups: Anglo-Saxons.

No-one is really sure why the Anglo-Saxons came to this country. It may have been because their land often flooded; it was difficult to grow crops, so they were looking for new places to settle down and farm. Some say that Saxon warriors were actually invited to come to Britain. By the end of the 6th century the Anglo-Saxons controlled most of southern Britain, which they began to call 'Angleland'.

These European settlers were not only great seamen and fierce fighters, but they were also excellent farmers. In Lewisham, the first areas attacked and then settled were probably along the River Ravensbourne, which could be navigated by small boats.

During the 9th, 10th and 11th centuries, Viking raids threatened the peace and stability of the region. The Vikings came from three countries in Scandinavia: Denmark; Norway; and Sweden. Vikings may have been fierce warriors but they, too, were mostly farmers, or worked as craftsmen or traders.

In 871AD, Deptford, which was then known as Meretun or 'Marsh Town', was the scene of a bloody battle. The Vikings fought with the Anglo-Saxon King Aethelred and his brother Alfred, who later became King Alfred the Great. The Anglo-Saxon brothers and their armies won that battle but lost the war... it would not be long before a Viking sat on the throne of England.

◄ Viking longship names were reflected in the shape of their prow: *Snake of the Sea* and *Horse of the Home of Ice* were popular choices

The Vikings demanded increasingly large sums of money called Danegeld to make them go away. In 1009, the people of Kent handed over £3,000, but two years later the bloodthirsty band returned, demanding more. Many people were killed and Alphege – the Archbishop of Canterbury – was taken hostage. He pleaded with the people not to pay a ransom for him and, later, was killed by his captors at a drunken feast in Greenwich.

More bloody battles followed until eventually, one of the Viking chiefs, Cnut, was crowned King of England in 1016.

When King Harold was defeated by William the Conqueror at the Battle of Hastings in 1066, it marked the end of Anglo-Saxon rule in this country. The Norman's succession to the English throne was the start of an exciting new chapter in this country's history.

▼ The Battle of Hastings in 1066 marked the start of Norman rule in Britain

BLACKHEATH

Blackheath was a wild and often dangerous place, covered with bushes and gorse and dotted with pits where gravel, chalk and limestone were dug out.

The heath itself used to be much larger, stretching from Blackheath Village to Kidbrooke. In 1432, King Henry VI granted a licence to the Duke of Gloucester to fence off, or 'enclose', 200 acres of the heath, which later became Greenwich Park. The heath was reduced in size further as people started to build grand houses around its edges. During the 19th century, roads were built across it, and the gorse and bushes cut down, to be replaced by grass.

Blackheath was within easy reach of the City of London and close to the Royal Palace at Greenwich, so it was often the scene of important historical events.

When the Peasants' Revolt took place in 1381, Wat Tyler and his 100,000-strong rebel army camped on the heath before they marched on London. In 1415, King Henry V, returning victorious from the Battle of Agincourt in France, was greeted on the heath by the Mayor and Aldermen of the City of London and a crowd of Londoners dressed in red and white.

Blackheath was again used as a meeting place for rebels when the supporters of Jack Cade gathered there in 1450. In 1497, 5,000 Cornishmen marched on the capital to protest to King Henry VII about unfair taxes. They were confronted by the king's army at Blackheath. Many of the rebels were killed and later buried on the heath, whilst their leaders surrendered and were hung, drawn and quartered.

The heath was also the site of the first meeting between King Henry VIII and his wife-to-be, Anne of Cleves, as well as Queen Elizabeth I's review of the City Militia.

The famous Methodist preachers John Wesley and George Whitefield addressed large crowds on the heath. John Wesley was a frequent visitor to Lewisham, staying with friends in the High Street. The mound George Whitefield preached on is often referred to as 'Whitefield's Mount' and may well be the burial site of the Cornish rebels!

From the 17th century onwards, fairs and markets were held twice a year on the heath, but they were stopped in the 19th century for being too rowdy. Perhaps too many people got drunk on the locally-brewed beer known as 'Peacock's Swipes'?

▶ The rebel armies led by Wat Tyler and John Ball march on London during the Peasants' Revolt

In the days before street lighting and proper roads, Blackheath could be a dangerous place. Many people were robbed at gunpoint by highwaymen. The situation got so bad that the citizens of the village put up a reward of £20 (a lot of money then) for catching a highwayman and £15 for a burglar.

Blackheath Village gives the impression of being quite old but, apart from the odd cottage, no houses were built there until the late 17th century. Old maps show that the village used to be called Dowager's Bottom! It was dominated by a large country estate called Wricklemarsh, with a huge mansion at its centre, said to be one of the finest in England. Many other large houses and villas were built in the 18th and 19th centuries. Some of the most famous and aristocratic people of their day lived there.

For centuries, the heath has been a popular venue for sport. The Royal Blackheath Golf Club claims to be the oldest in England. It is quite possible that King James I played on the Blackheath course, which was only five holes' long. The gravel pits made great natural bunkers! Blackheath is also home to the world's oldest rugby club, Blackheath Football Club (Rugby Union), which was founded in 1858.

◀ A 19th century view of the road from Blackheath to Lewisham

TIME TRAVELLERS

For many hundreds of years, sailors have navigated around the world using maps based on an invisible grid of lines of longitude and latitude. The equator – latitude 0 – separates the northern and southern hemispheres, whilst the prime meridian – longitude 0 – separates the eastern and western hemispheres. If you know your longitude and latitude, you can pinpoint exactly where you are in the world. It's the same principle as the satellite navigation systems we use today.

When Christopher Columbus sailed across the Atlantic in 1492, there was no reliable way of measuring a ship's longitude once out of sight of land. Much of the world remained unexplored

▼ Planisphere world map published around 1508

and maps were often inaccurate or incomplete. As a result, voyages frequently took longer than expected and could end in disaster if a ship got lost or ran aground. Some countries offered large rewards to anyone who could find an accurate way of measuring longitude at sea. And Britain came up with two winning solutions!

As early as 1514, people realised that the moon could be used as a 'clock' for measuring longitude. In 1675, a Royal Observatory was built at Greenwich to explore this idea... and 91 years later someone came up with a solution. That person was the Astronomer Royal, Nevil Maskelyne. He published the first Nautical Almanac, a table of figures showing the position of the moon and other bright stars at different times of the day. Using these numbers, and a nautical instrument known as a sextant, British sailors could accurately calculate their longitude.

The second solution came from an English clockmaker, John Harrison. He managed to build a watch so accurate and reliable that it could be used to measure longitude to the nearest half degree. He won the colossal sum of £20,000 for his efforts, which shows how important people considered his invention to be.

▲ John Harrison's award-winning longitude watch

For many years, countries measured longitude using different meridians. Finally, in 1884, an international conference in Washington DC decided that the position of a special telescope called the Airy Transit Circle at the Greenwich Observatory should be the location of the world's prime meridian. It made sense, as two-thirds of ships were already using charts based on the Greenwich Meridian. This prime meridian passes through Lewisham on its journey to the North and South Poles and back!

It was also agreed at the conference that time should be measured from Greenwich, which gave us Greenwich Mean Time. All the countries of the world fit roughly into a grid of 24 time zones, each 15 degrees of longitude wide and an hour apart. For example, when it's 1pm in Greenwich, it's 2pm in France and 3pm in Greece.

Some countries, such as the USA, Australia and Russia, are so big that they cross several time zones, which means the time will be different depending on where you are in the country. How confusing is that? Some also make use of Summer Time, or Daylight Saving Time, when clocks are put forward in the spring and back again in the autumn.

▼ The Royal Observatory at Greenwich is located on longitide 0 – the prime meridian

BROCKLEY

In early times, much of Brockley was covered by woodland. By the 18th century most of the trees had been cut down to make way for farms, fields and market gardens.

An abbey was established in the area around 1187, near the present St Peter's Church in Wickham Road.

In 1800, Brockley was a rural settlement on an old lane that ran from Deptford to Sydenham. Brockley village was located in what is now known as Crofton Park. It had a few large houses, tumbledown cottages, rustic inns and a pleasant village green. During the 19th century, the fields and market gardens were gradually built over, creating street after street of new houses.

Many of the street names we see today come from two families who owned much of the land in Brockley in the 18th century. The Wickham family married into the Drake family of Shardeloes, Buckinghamshire, and later changed their name to Tyrwhitt-Drake.

Brockley Hall, which was originally a farm house, became home to the Noakes family, who were Bermondsey brewers. The last of the line was Maude Noakes, who kept a menagerie of pets there. Builders were eager to develop the estate and, within a year of her death in 1931, had constructed Brockley Hall Road on the site.

The Noakes sold their beer at the Brockley Jack pub. The old wooden building had an inn sign made out of the shoulder blade of a whale. There are stories that the notorious highwayman, Dick Turpin, used to frequent the old Brockley Jack tavern. But this could be a landlord's tall tale! The tavern was replaced by the present building in 1898.

One of Brockley's best-known residents was the Irishman 'Big' Jim Connell. He wrote the Labour Party's traditional anthem 'The Red Flag' in 1889 on the train home from Charing Cross to New Cross.

▶ The old Brockley Jack with its inn sign made from the shoulder bone of a whale

13

ON THE MOVE

Before trains and cars, people relied on horses and their own two feet to get them from place to place. With the area covered mostly by farms and fields, most roads in the borough were little more than muddy, pot-holed tracks.

Things began to improve with the establishment of tollgates. The money paid by travellers was used to keep the roads in good repair. There were five tollgates in the borough: New Cross Road; Evelyn Street; Eltham Road; Lewisham High Street; and Newlands Park. All were removed in the 1860s, after which travel by road was free.

Until the 1830s, the stagecoach was the only form of public transport in the borough. In 1836, London's first railway line opened, running from Spa Road, Bermondsey (extended soon afterwards to London Bridge) to Deptford. The track was carried on a viaduct of 878 arches. Many people at the time thought they would collapse, but they are still in use today.

The next line to open in Lewisham was the London to Croydon railway in 1839, passing through New Cross, Forest Hill and Sydenham. The North Kent to Gravesend line opened in 1849, via Lewisham and Blackheath, and the Lewisham to Beckenham line in 1857, via Ladywell and Lower Sydenham. The Lewisham to Dartford line was opened in 1866, via Lee and, finally, the Nunhead to Shortlands line in 1892, via Catford and Bellingham. The coming of the railways transformed places in the borough from rural communities into towns and suburbs.

Horse-drawn buses provided an alternative means of transport from the mid-19th century. Thomas Tilling operated many bus routes in the area and his company had a depot in Old Road, Lee, where the horses were stabled. Tilling started operating motor buses from 1904, which soon replaced the horse-drawn ones. In time, he sold his business to London Transport.

▼ The atmospheric railway in 1840, a pioneering 'green' transport scheme (see page 53)

◀ The Deptford & Greenwich Railway, from the Surrey Canal, dated 1840

Lewisham used to have two canals: the Croydon and the Grand Surrey. The Croydon Canal was 9.5 miles long and ran from New Cross, where it joined with the Grand Surrey Canal, to Croydon via Brockley, Forest Hill and Sydenham. The canal was a financial failure, both through lack of demand from businesses and the fact that it had to climb a steep slope between New Cross and Forest Hill, requiring 26 locks over a distance of 2.5 miles. It closed in 1836 and was bought by the London to Croydon Railway Company, who built their new train line along much of its route.

The Grand Surrey Canal suffered a similar fate. It opened in 1807 and was originally intended to reach Kingston and Epsom in Surrey, but it only got as far as Peckham! The canal stayed in use until the 1970s.

▼ The Croydon Canal at Sydenham

The first horse-drawn trams operated from New Cross Gate to Greenwich via Deptford from 1870. They ran on rails buried in the road. Shortly after, other tramlines were built between Lewisham and Catford. By 1907, all the horse-drawn trams had been replaced by electric ones, either taking power from overhead wires or a third rail buried in the road beside the tracks.

In the early years of the 20th century, the tramlines were extended to Lee, Brockley, Forest Hill, Grove Park and Southend. But they became too expensive to run and were scrapped after the Second World War. The last tram ran from Woolwich to the big tram depot at New Cross in 1952. This depot is now used by buses.

CATFORD

Catford became a manor in its own right when parts of the old manor of Lewisham were sold off some time before 1291.

There were two huge, moated mansions in the town: Rushey Green Place, located near today's Ringstead Road; and Manor House, located near Catford Bridge station. Rushey Green Place was once the home of William Hatcliffe. The Pope's special representative, Cardinal Campeggio, stayed there in 1518. He was later involved in King Henry VIII's negotiations with the Catholic Church over his divorce from Catherine of Aragon.

Catford remained a small farming community until the 19th century. The land was boggy and often flooded after heavy rain: the name Rushey Green comes from the fact that rushes grew there.

Better roads and access into the City of London led to a rapid growth in stagecoach travel during the 18th and early 19th centuries. Large inns were built to accommodate the stagecoaches, their passengers and horses. Popular inns in Catford included the Black Horse and Harrow, George Inn and Rising Sun. During the 19th century, stagecoach travel declined as the railways grew in importance.

The Victorian period was a time of significant improvement in towns and cities. But many continued to be very smelly, and Catford was no exception. For centuries, people disposed of their rubbish and the contents of their toilets on the streets and in the rivers. The rapid growth in low cost housing only added to the problem. So, in 1855-56, a large sewer was built under Rushey Green, which brought considerable 'relief' to the local residents! Gas street lighting was also installed, to be replaced by electric lighting in the 1930s.

It seems the people of Catford really enjoyed their leisure time. The River Ravensbourne was then wide and deep enough for swimming and boating. In 1908 the new roller-skating craze hit the town, with the opening of the Roller-skating Hall near the corner of Sangley Road. A year later, Catford's first cinema – the Electric Picture Palace – opened nearby. It would eventually be joined by two others. 1911 saw the opening of the Hippodrome Theatre on the corner of Brownhill Road and Rushey Green – London's largest music hall at the time. The Lewisham Concert Hall, now Lewisham Theatre, was opened in 1932, the same year as the Catford Stadium greyhound track. The town also had a national cycling arena for a short time.

Like many places in London, Catford suffered serious bomb damage during the Second World War. New buildings emerged from the rubble and the town grew in importance as a shopping centre.

PAUPERS' PALACE?

During the late 18th and early 19th centuries, there was a huge increase in the number of poor people. Many had left the countryside to work in the towns, but there were not enough jobs for them all. A number of towns had already created institutions where the poorest people could live. But, in 1834, it was made compulsory for parishes to join together in groups called Unions, and for each Union to have its own 'workhouse'.

Workhouses provided accommodation for the poorest people who could not afford their own homes or to look after themselves. They were deliberately intended to be unpleasant places, so that only the most desperate people would want to stay. Men and women were separated, the food was bad, and there were strict rules preventing people from leaving the workhouse or from having visitors. The diet was very boring, changing little from day to day: porridge for breakfast; thin soup for lunch; and bread and cheese for supper. However, on special days such as Christmas and Easter, the residents got better food, like beef and plum pudding!

There had been a workhouse in Lewisham since at least the 1740s. By the beginning of the 19th century it was in a poor state and a new one was built in 1817 in Rushey Green. There were also two workhouses in Deptford until the 1840s.

◄ More!! The famous workhouse scene from Charles Dickens' *Oliver Twist*

Some poor people were also helped by the parish in their own homes with gifts of money, clothing, food or coal.

The conditions in Lewisham workhouse were pretty bad. Because of the poor diet, children often suffered from diseases such as rickets, anaemia and skin infections. It did not help that they had to sleep three or four to a bed! The building was overcrowded, poorly ventilated and cold in the winter. Adults worked mainly at oakum-picking, which involved pulling out the fibres in old ropes. This was used by shipbuilders to fill in the gaps between the planks of ships to make them watertight.

By the 1850s, the majority of those forced into the workhouse were old, sick, orphaned, unmarried mothers and physically and mentally ill people. Conditions did start to improve towards the end of the 19th century. New institutions were created to look after the sick, orphaned children and those with a mental disability. Life became a little easier for the workhouse residents, with more varied food, small 'luxuries' such as books and newspapers and the occasional outing.

During the First World War, part of the Lewisham workhouse was used as a military hospital. The residents were transferred to other institutions. Some of the older people were not moved until later, when the workhouse building became part of Lewisham Hospital. Workhouses were finally abolished by the Government in 1930.

▶ Bermondsey Union Workshouse at Ladywell

19

DEPTFORD

The medieval inhabitants of Deptford mostly earned a living as fishermen, shipbuilders and river pilots.

The land by the River Thames was marshy and liable to flood, so there's been a bridge across the River Ravensbourne at Deptford Creek since at least the early Middle Ages. A watermill stood in the Creek and there were other mills nearby on the banks of the River Thames, used for grinding corn. Beyond the shore lay fields and woods.

There used to be a real green at Deptford Green. St Nicholas' Church, whose rather creepy entrance is flanked by the skull and crossbones, has stood there since the Middle Ages. The church is dedicated to the patron saint of sailors (and Christmas). It is also known as 'the Westminster Abbey of the Navy' or the 'Admirals' Church', as so many seafarers worshipped there before setting off on their long and often dangerous voyages.

The famous playwright Christopher Marlowe was buried in the churchyard after his mysterious death in a pub fight in the town in 1593. Christopher's plays had a huge influence on Elizabethan theatre. William Shakespeare was certainly inspired by his work. Some experts even suggest that many of Shakespeare's plays were actually written by Marlowe. Some also believe that Christopher was a government secret agent!

John Evelyn, another popular author of his time, lived at Sayes Court in the late 17th century and, like his contemporary Samuel Pepys, kept a diary. Evelyn's writings give us a lot of insight into the daily life of a gentleman in Stuart England. He created a beautiful garden at his house, which stood near where Sayes Court Recreation Ground is located today. Peter the Great, Tsar of Russia, came to stay in 1698, so that he could learn the art of shipbuilding. Unfortunately, the Tsar and his friends trashed the house and gardens, smashing furniture, ruining carpets and slashing pictures. He was not invited back!

Until the early years of the 19th century, Deptford High Street was just a leafy country lane called Butt Lane, wending its way through fields and market gardens. The Broadway was a green with a well in the middle.

Apart from shipbuilding, there were many other industries in Deptford, including brass and iron foundries, potteries, breweries, saw mills, flour mills and heavy engineering. But the key to Deptford's fortunes – and later misfortunes – was the Royal Naval Dockyard, established by King Henry VIII in 1513. Within 30 years,

▶ The *Royal George* anchored off Deptford and the launch of the *Cambridge*

21

Deptford had become the most important naval shipyard in England. There was plenty of work for the sailors, shipbuilders, carpenters, ropemakers and other tradesmen who settled there. They mostly lived in small wooden cottages, but there were also shops and one or two grand houses... as well as over 100 pubs!

King Edward VI came to watch a mock sea battle at Deptford in 1549. His half sister, Queen Elizabeth I, dined there in 1581 with Sir Francis Drake on board his ship, the Golden Hind, and later watched him being knighted. Drake had sailed around the world in the little ship. Afterwards, it was moored at Deptford as a tourist attraction, rather like the Cutty Sark at Greenwich. Sadly, by 1662, it had rotted and had to be broken up.

War with Spain in the 1580s and 1590s kept the dockyard busy and, in 1587, the Ark Royal, the flagship of the fleet that fought the Spanish Armada, was launched from there. In the 1650s England went to war with Holland, which meant more work for Deptford. Samuel Pepys, who was a member of the Navy Board, often came to the town to inspect the dockyard. By the end of the 17th century, England was at war with France, and Deptford continued to prosper. The boom period carried on into the 18th century, which saw, on average, a war every ten years. Deptford dockyard struggled to keep up with the demand for war ships.

However, by the early 19th century, the dockyard was facing serious problems. The River Thames was silting up, making it difficult to launch big ships. Furthermore, Britain was largely at peace with its neighbours, so demand for vessels fell. Finally, in 1869, the Royal Naval Dockyard closed for good. Many people lost their jobs. Some sailed to America or Australia to start a new life.

The dockyard site was taken over by the Foreign Cattle Market. Girls who worked there were known as 'gut girls' because they had the horrible job of cleaning out the carcasses of the cows and sheep, working in filthy conditions. It closed in 1913.

The Royal Victualling Yard next to the dockyard stayed open until the 1960s. It made and stored supplies for the Navy, such as rum, biscuits, salted beef and pork, chocolate and soap. The Pepys estate was built on part of the site and the old rum warehouses by the river converted into flats, a sailing centre and a library.

Other famous maritime institutions also based themselves at Deptford: Trinity House, which started as a medieval seamen's guild and is now the UK's navigational authority; the East India Company, which was formed as a trading company in 1600; and the General Steam Navigation Company, which built paddle steamers at the mouth of Deptford Creek.

The 20th century was a rather depressing chapter in Deptford's proud history. The town suffered badly during the depression of the 1930s and was heavily bombed in the Second World War. However, it has seen significant regeneration in recent years.

VENUS & BOUNTY

In the 18th century, the Pacific Ocean was still virtually uncharted. For centuries there had been rumours of a great southern continent. French, Dutch and English sailors, including Francis Drake, had all searched in vain for this mythical land.

The British Admiralty decided to organise a scientific expedition to the southern hemisphere to observe the movement of the planet Venus, which would eclipse the sun in June 1769. In this new age of science and discovery, mathematicians could use the measurements to calculate the distance between the earth and the sun. The expedition would also have a secret mission... to locate the great southern continent!

The Admiralty chose a brilliant young navigator called James Cook to lead the mission. He took charge of HMS Endeavour at Deptford, filling it with limes (to prevent the deadly disease scurvy), along with ship's biscuits, rum and other stores from the Victualling Yard (it only became *Royal* in 1858 after it was visited by Queen Victoria!).

The Endeavour sailed to Tahiti and gifts were exchanged with the friendly natives, who agreed to let the scientists set up their measuring equipment on the island. After successfully plotting the movement of Venus, Cook continued his journey. But there

▲ The death of Captain Cook in 1779, from an unfinished painting

was no sign of the great southern continent, though they did reach New Zealand, where Cook was the first person to map the coastline. They sailed back along the coast of eastern Australia, the first Europeans to see it, and Cook drew more maps. He returned to England via the East Indies and was welcomed back as a hero.

Cook undertook two more voyages on behalf of the Admiralty, but he never found the great southern continent. On his second voyage, he used the new maritime clock developed by John Harrison to determine his exact position. On his third voyage, to find the North-West Passage believed to link the Atlantic and Pacific Oceans, Cook ended up in Hawaii. There, he was treated like a god by the islanders. However, the mood changed when

Cook tried to take the Hawaiian king hostage after the theft of a boat. There was a fight, and Cook was stabbed and died on 14 February, 1779.

Just over 40 years later, the Russian Fabian Gottlieb von Bellingshausen became the first person to see the coast of Antarctica, the great southern continent.

William Bligh was sailing master on HMS Resolution for Cook's third voyage around the world. After Cook's death, the expedition returned to England.

Bligh was given command of a merchant ship and moved his family to Wapping. In 1787, he was appointed Captain of a ship that would change his life forever. The Bounty was fitted out at Deptford for the transportation of breadfruit plants from Tahiti to the plantations in the West Indies.

Bligh and his crew spent six months on Tahiti as they prepared for their long voyage to the Caribbean. But a number of crew members had become friendly with the local native women and did not want to leave the tropical paradise. Bligh's second in command, Fletcher Christian, and some of the crew, mutinied. The Captain and 18 men loyal to him were

▲ The mutineers cast William Bligh and loyal officers and crew adrift

cast adrift in a small boat. They drifted 4,000 miles before running aground at Timor. Bligh finally arrived back in England in 1790.

He was not blamed for the loss of the Bounty and was given command of a second breadfruit expedition and two ships: HMS Providence and the Assistant, both also fitted out at Deptford. His next expedition was a success and Bligh returned to London with a Tahitian called Mydiddee, who wanted to see the land of King George III. Sadly, Mydiddee died just as they arrived back in England and was buried in St Paul's churchyard in Deptford.

Bligh lived in Sydenham in 1812 and died five years later. Many Tahitians today can trace their ancestry back to the Bounty's mutineers.

FOREST HILL & HONOR OAK

It's not hard to guess how Forest Hill got its name. For hundreds of years its inhabitants used wood from the forest for charcoal-burning and as fuel for their fires and grazed their pigs there.

By the mid-18th century, nearly all the trees in Westwood Forest had been cut down, to be replaced by fields, and the local people turned to farming for a living.

Queen Elizabeth I is said to have paid a visit to her friend Sir Richard Bulkley at Lewisham on May Day in 1602. They had a picnic together under the shade of an oak tree between Forest Hill and Brockley. This led to it being called the 'oak of honour'. In time, the area became known as Honor Oak.

In 1809, the Croydon Canal, which ran from New Cross to Croydon, was opened. Its route took it alongside Devonshire Road. There was a stable for the horses that pulled the barges in Stanstead Road. It may not have been a financial success, but the canal and the reservoir at Sydenham Park were popular with local people, who used them for boating, fishing, skating and picnics.

As with most other places in the borough, the coming of the railway led to a huge growth in house-building. Large houses were built for middle-class families, as well as smaller terraced houses for working-class people, many of whom were employed as servants in the big houses. With the building of the Crystal Palace in nearby Sydenham, Forest Hill became a very popular place to live.

By the outbreak of the First World War, the town was completely built-up. It even had its own visitor attraction, Horniman's Museum, which was opened in 1901 by tea merchant Frederick Horniman. Forest Hill seems to have held a particular attraction for tea merchants – Mr Tetley also lived there!

During the 20th century, parts of Forest Hill changed beyond recognition. Many of the large houses were pulled down and replaced by modern houses or blocks of flats.

One elderly resident wrote to the local newspaper in 1929 to say that he still remembered the 'good old days' when the tradesmen in Dartmouth Road included a blacksmith, Mr Boodle, who mended cane chairs, Duffin's Dairy, which kept its cows in a small field behind the shop, and Mr Brown the chimney sweep!

THE PEOPLE'S MUSEUM

Frederick Horniman inherited the family tea business from his father, John, who was a prominent member of the religious sect known as Quakers. Even in the early years of Queen Victoria's reign there was still prejudice against Quakers – they weren't allowed to go to university, for example – so many became businessmen. John chose tea as his career, setting himself up as a merchant in 1826. He was one of the first to sell leaf tea in foil-lined packets. The business prospered and Horniman Pure Tea became a household name.

John was an enthusiastic traveller who loved to collect strange and exotic objects on his many journeys. His love of travel and unusual objects was shared by his son Frederick, who added to his father's collections from his travels in Europe, North Africa, the Far East and America.

Frederick was a small man, but he had a lot of energy. In addition to running the family tea business, he was a Member of the London County Council and the MP for Falmouth in Cornwall.

If you asked Frederick the secret of his success his

◀ A rather over-stuffed walrus in the Natural History Gallery at Horniman's Museum

answer might have been 'rice pudding'. He loved it and always took plenty with him on his long journeys to Cornwall! He was a very generous man and gave a lot of his time and money to good causes.

Frederick did not actually start travelling abroad until he was 59. His special interests included natural history, archaeology, anthropology and musical instruments, but he also liked to collect everyday objects that showed how civilisations around the world had evolved. Frederick's friends knew about his many interests and often gave him objects they had collected on their own travels.

Frederick opened up part of his home in Forest Hill to the public, so they could see the objects he had collected. Though busy, he still found time to show visitors around his little museum. Soon his collections became so large that they filled the whole house, and he decided to create a proper museum for them.

Frederick got one of the leading architects of the day, Charles Harrison Townsend, to design his museum. It opened in 1901. His old house, Surrey Mount, became a tearoom and its gardens became the Horniman Gardens. Frederick generously gave the new museum and its grounds as a free gift to the people of London for their 'recreation, instruction and enjoyment'.

He always had a special affection for children and parties from schools, children's homes and orphanages were warmly welcomed and often given free lemonade and cakes to make their visit extra special.

The original museum collections included natural history specimens, cultural objects and musical instruments. Further buildings were added to the museum, including one paid for by Frederick's son Emslie in 1911, who also added to the collections from his own travels. Emslie provided the money to build the library and lecture hall and left a considerable sum to the museum when he died.

Over the last 100 years the museum has enlarged its collections significantly. Frederick's original gift accounts for just a small proportion of today's exhibits. A new extension and other spaces were opened in 2002.

The Horniman Museum is one of Forest Hill's major attractions and now welcomes over 750,000 visitors every year.

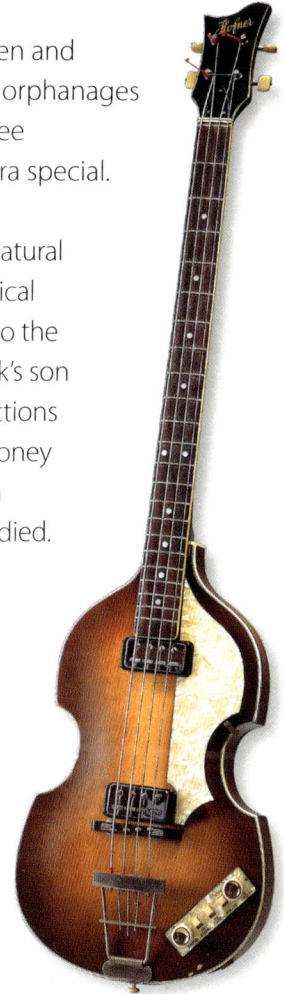

▲ The Horniman butterfly discovered and named by Frederick Horniman

▶ The Hohner bass guitar made famous by Paul McCartney of *The Beatles*

GROVE PARK

Grove Park's earliest days are very much like those of Forest Hill's, the majority of the area being covered with woodland until it was later developed for farmland. The area's name probably comes from Grove Farm, which was located alongside what is now Baring Road.

Much of the land in Grove Park was owned by the Baring family, Lords of the manor of Lee. There were several farms, including Claypit Farm, so called because clay was dug there during the 19th century and sent to a pottery in Greenwich to be made into sugar-loaf moulds.

Grove Park remained an isolated farming community until the late 19th century, when Grove Park railway station was opened.

Between 1899 and 1902 a workhouse for people from Greenwich was built in Marvels Lane. It provided accommodation for over 750 people. Local people thought the building was too large and extravagant for a workhouse so they nicknamed it the 'Paupers' Palace'!

When the First World War broke out in 1914, the residents of the workhouse were moved and the buildings occupied by the Army Service Corps (ASC). During the war, Grove Park's streets were teeming with lorries, ambulances and armoured cars awaiting despatch to the battlefields in France. There were also two large camps for the ASC men.

Local people welcomed the soldiers into their homes and the then Lord of the Manor, Lord Northbrooke, lent out one of his houses in Baring Road as a social club, which was free to soldiers and sailors in uniform.

Before the First World War, Grove Park was quite a prosperous area, with many large houses, some of which had tennis courts or swimming pools. It was separated from the more built-up areas of the borough by a strip of countryside and orchards.

During the late 1920s, the huge Grove Park estate was built to meet the growing demand from local people for better quality, low cost housing in the borough.

After the Second World War, many of the large houses were demolished or turned into flats and more Council estates were built. Grove Park may have lost its rural character, but it's still one of the quieter areas of the borough.

BOMBING BLITZ

Like most of inner London, Lewisham received a terrible pounding from German bombers during the Second World War. The borough lay directly under the flight paths of enemy bombers approaching or returning from the City of London and the docks. In addition, V1 and V2 flying bombs aimed at central London often fell short of their intended targets.

The worst period of bombing was known as the Blitz, when there were enemy raids nearly every night from September 1940 until May 1941. However, the most serious bomb incidents in Lewisham happened later in the war. Sandhurst Road School in Catford took a direct hit on 20 January, 1943 and 38 children and six teachers were killed. During the same raid, German planes flew low and machine-gunned people in the streets.

A V1 flying bomb landed in Lewisham town centre on 28 July, 1944, killing over 50 people and injuring nearly 300. A V2 rocket attack killed 52 people in Trundleys Road, Deptford on 7 March, 1945. But the worst V2 rocket attack happened on 25 November, 1944, when a busy Woolworths store in New Cross Road was totally destroyed. This was the most deadly of all three raids: 160 people were killed and 108 taken to hospital, many of them children shopping for sweets after a swim at the public baths.

▶ Thousands of Lewisham children were evacuated to the country to escape the air raids

Over 2,000 Lewisham civilians lost their lives during the war and more than 8,000 were injured. Thousands more were killed or injured fighting overseas. The bombing caused widespread damage. Over 68,000 people were made homeless and 4,600 homes destroyed; many others were badly damaged, along with schools, shops, churches and public buildings.

When an air raid took place a siren would sound and people ran for cover in specially constructed shelters. Anderson shelters were steel huts partially buried in back gardens and covered with earth. Morrison shelters were large steel cages that were placed under tables. There were also a number of public shelters, including a series under Lewisham street market, which provided safety for shoppers and local residents. At night, people took it in turns to fire-watch – looking out for the small incendiary bombs that could set fire to buildings if not extinguised.

Thousands of Lewisham men and women served in the armed forces. Many thousands more worked in munitions and armaments factories, or on farms or in coal mines, to replace the men who had gone to war. Civilians at home had to serve in the Home Guard, Fire Service, Civil Defence or Women's Volunteer Service, in addition to their regular jobs.

By early 1941, more than 80,000 people had been evacuated from Lewisham to escape the air raids. Local children were sent away to safe places in the country, living with strangers in Wales and Sussex, amongst other places, until it was safe to return home.

Many convoys of merchant ships bringing food into the country were attacked and some foods became scarce. Rationing started in January, 1940. Each person was only allowed four ounces (113g) of bacon, four ounces (113g) of butter and 12 ounces (340g) of sugar a week. Sweets were also rationed! Some foods, like eggs, oranges, lemons and bananas, became very scarce or even impossible to get.

The war – and the redevelopment afterwards – changed the face of the borough forever.

▶ The V1 rocket attack on Lewisham town centre in 1944 killed over 50 people and injured nearly 300

HITHER GREEN

Hither Green is situated on the site of a hamlet known in the Middle Ages as Romborough. It was still largely countryside until the end of the 19th century and Hither Green Lane and Verdant Lane, as their names imply, were just country tracks.

A number of large houses were built in the area, including one called Mountsfield. When the house was demolished in 1905, its gardens were turned into Mountsfield Park. Brownhill Road and St Mildred's Road were built in the 1880s, but not at the same time. That's why there's a bend where the roads meet under the railway bridge. It's fortunate that the builders of the Channel Tunnel did not have the same problem!

The railway arrived relatively late to the area in 1895, when Hither Green station was opened. But the person who really changed the face of the town was a scotsman called Archibald Cameron Corbett.

In 1896, Corbett bought 278 acres of farmland. Over the next 17 years, he built over 3,000 houses on the land. They were quite large, with three to six bedrooms, solidly constructed and attractive to look at. The houses are still popular today and have become known as 'Corbett' houses. When they were first sold, prices ranged from £248 to £488!

Corbett strongly disapproved of drinking, which is why there are no pubs on the estate. He named many of the streets after places in his native Scotland, including Ardgowan, Torridon, Muirkirk and Glenfarg.

Hither Green's Park Hospital was opened in 1897. Many trees grow behind its high walls, including the largest Bean tree in the UK. When the hospital closed, new homes were built on the site. Some old buildings – like the water tower – have been kept.

In the far corner of Hither Green cemetery is Railway Children Walk, named in memory of the author Edith Nesbit, who lived in Baring Road in Grove Park. Also in the cemetery is a mass grave for the tragic victims of the Second World War bomb attack on Catford's Sandhurst Road School.

Hither Green Library (now called Torridon Road Library) was opened in 1907, but to begin with had no books... the Council couldn't afford to buy any until the following year! By 1910, the Corbett estate had shops, four schools and six churches.

In 1967 there was a tragic rail accident just outside Hither Green station. A train was derailed because of a faulty track and 49 people were killed.

SLAVES & MASTERS

You may think that a multi-ethnic London is a relatively recent development, but black people have lived here since Roman times. Archaeological evidence shows that there were Africans among the ranks of the invading Roman legions. The River Thames was an important route for the conquering Romans, as it was for later incoming Africans.

Among the musicians at the court of King Henry VII was a black trumpeter called John Blanke. This was almost certainly a nickname, as the name Blanke means white! But John Blanke was not a slave – he was paid eight pence a day to play.

Kings and Queens were very much the celebrities of their day and played a crucial role in promoting new ideas and fashions. When Catherine of Aragon arrived at Deptford from Spain to marry Henry VII's eldest son Arthur, her staff included two African slaves. Spanish trade in African slaves was already well established: a steady supply of labour was needed to work on the plantations in Spain's West Indian colonies.

The resulting wars with Spain and France, following King Henry VIII's marriage to Catherine and subsequent divorce, had a major impact on the growth of the black community in Lewisham. At the core of this was the establishment of the Royal Naval Dockyard at Deptford and Britain's growing importance as the dominant, global seapower. Deptford soon attracted a network of adventurers and their wealthy financial backers, who were keen to take advantage of the highly profitable trade triangle between Britain, Africa and the West Indies.

William Hawkins and his son John were early pioneers of the African slave trade in London. They were soon joined by other well-known seafarers of the day. Martin Frobisher, better known for his voyages to the Arctic, joined the first fleet to sail to Benin in West Africa. Francis Drake sailed alongside John Hawkins on a slaving expedition in 1568. A year later, another business associate of Hawkins, Walter Raleigh, recruited volunteers for his crew at Deptford.

With the success of these slaving activities, black people were brought back to London as slaves, servants and even gifts. They were later joined by black former soldiers who had fought for the British during the American War of Independence, with the promise of freedom for their loyalty and service.

The slave trade continued to prosper, as did the financial backers and merchants, many of whom occupied some of the grandest houses in the borough.

Not only did black people become more visible during the latter part of the 18th century, but they also became more vocal.

Olaudah Equiano, for example, who was kidnapped in what is now Nigeria when he was 11, wrote a vivid account of his life as a slave. After buying his freedom in 1766 for £40, Olaudah went on to become a leading black figure, championing the cause of freedom by giving talks on the horrors of slavery across the country.

Calls for slavery to be abolished grew louder during the late 18th and early 19th centuries, but campaigners faced heavy opposition: trade in slaves had become integral to the economy of the country and was well protected by the legal system.

In 1787, the Society for the Abolition of the Slave Trade was formed, with the MP William Wilberforce as its spokesman. The Society distributed anti-slavery leaflets and stirred up public opinion against the slave trade. Other anti-slavery societies sprung up all over the country, including a prominent one at Hatcham led by Joseph Hardcastle. The efforts of these campaigners finally succeeded with the passing of the Slave Trade Act in 1807, ending 300 years of black exploitation.

Although numbers dwindled during the 19th century, black Londoners from Africa and, increasingly, the Caribbean were still very much a part of community life. In Lewisham, the majority worked as seamen or in the dockyards and neighbouring businesses.

Even into the 20th century, black people faced discrimination in pubs and boarding houses, as well as on the streets.

On 22 June, 1948, the merchant vessel Empire Windrush arrived in England with the first group of post-war immigrants from the Caribbean. Of the 492 passengers on board, seven gave a forwarding address in Lewisham.

Like most places in London with a large ethnic community, problems sometimes arose in the borough over issues of housing, employment and policing. The death of 14 black youngsters at a party in New Cross in January 1981 led to a Black People's Day of Action, the largest protest march organised by black people in British history.

Such unrest is virtually unheard of these days. Lewisham benefits from being one of the most culturally diverse boroughs in London. It has welcomed immigrants from every continent for centuries and will continue to do so... a real cause for celebration!

THE NEGRO SERVANT; AN AUTHENTIC AND INTERESTING NARRATIVE OF A YOUNG NEGRO.

◀ Conditions on board the slave ships were appalling and many died on the long journey

LADYWELL

Ladywell gets its name from the well which must have been associated with the parish church of Lewisham in some way, being dedicated to St Mary the Virgin (our Lady).

There used to be a wooden bridge for pedestrians over the River Ravensbourne at Ladywell; horses and carts simply drove through the shallow water. It was replaced by a brick bridge in 1830.

Lewisham vicarage, which was built in 1692-3, still stands at the corner of Ladywell Road and Lewisham High Street. Opposite the vicarage was a large mansion called Lewisham House, where Sir John Lethieullier and his wife Lady Anne lived in the late 17th century. Samuel Pepys clearly knew the family well, as he wrote about Lady Anne in his diary: '...our noble fat brave lady in our parish, that I and my wife admire so'. I wonder how Lady Anne reacted to such a 'compliment'?

The Lewisham School of Industry was established nearby in Lewisham High Street in 1795 to train working class children for useful employment. Lewisham children were sometimes 'acquired' by Lancashire and Yorkshire manufacturers to serve as apprentices, although they were often treated more like slaves!

Along what is now Ladywell Road lay the fields of Slagrave and Bridge House farms. By the 1840s, a few cottages had been built along the road, but most of the building work took place after the railway station was opened in 1857.

One of the fields was turned into Ladywell and Brockley Cemetery a year later and in 1889 more farmland was taken to create a public park, Ladywell Recreation Ground.

In 1894 Slagrave Farm was sold and a new workhouse for Bermondsey people built on the land. The workhouse was just for old people and it was less grim than some of the others. Most of the workhouse, which was later renamed Ladywell Lodge, has now been demolished, but other accommodation for elderly and disabled people has been built on the site.

Blackheath-born Emily Davison addressed large gatherings of suffragettes from the top of Hilly Fields, demanding equal voting rights for women. She later threw herself under the king's horse on Derby Day in 1913 in protest at the treatment of suffragettes in prison.

By the beginning of the 20th century all the farmland in Ladywell had disappeared under streets of houses.

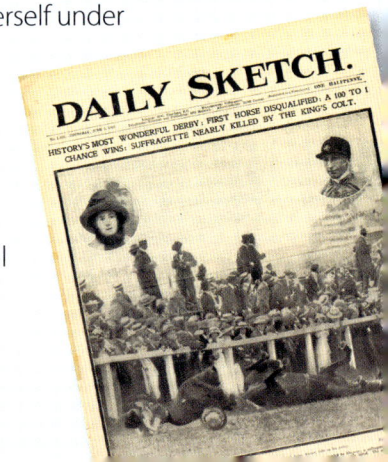

DAILY SKETCH.

HISTORY'S MOST WONDERFUL DERBY: FIRST HORSE DISQUALIFIED; A 100 TO 1 CHANCE WINS: SUFFRAGETTE NEARLY KILLED BY THE KING'S COLT.

PARISH PATTER

A parish is an area served by a particular church. The borough of Lewisham used to be divided into three parishes: St Mary's, Lewisham; St Margaret's, Lee; and St Paul's, Deptford.

In the Middle Ages, the parish church in Lewisham stood where St Mary's is now, but it was much smaller. The ceiling was ornately decorated with clouds and stars. Men and women sat on opposite sides of the church!

By the 1770s, the building was in a poor state, so it was rebuilt. Only the lower part of the tower, dating from the late 15th century, remains today. Unfortunately, there was a fire on Boxing Day in 1830, which damaged part of the building and destroyed many of the parish records. Those records that did survive the fire contain some interesting entries, including the burial of James Glover in 1740 '...*killed at Sipenham* (Sydenham) *by a pitch fork*'.

The most famous vicar of Lewisham was Rev. Abraham Colfe, who lived from 1580 to 1657. Not only did Colfe found Colfe's Grammar School, but he also built six almshouses for old people, which used to stand next to Lewisham Hospital. When he died, Colfe left a very long will, which included many gifts to the poor.

▲ St Mary's at Lewisham, from an 1870 painting

The old church of St Margaret's at Lee was demolished in 1813, also to make way for a larger building. So many people were moving into Lee that even the new church quickly became too small and an even larger church was built on the opposite side of the road in 1841. You can still see the remains of the tower of the old church and some crumbling tombstones in the churchyard across the road.

▲ St Paul's at Deptford, from an 1835 painting

Edmund Halley, who died in 1854, is buried in St Margaret's churchyard. He was Astronomer Royal at the Greenwich Observatory and gave his name to Halley's Comet. Another less well-known person buried at Lee is Robert Cocking, who died in 1837. Cocking thought he had invented the parachute. He was proved wrong when he jumped from a hot air balloon into a field at Burnt Ash and was killed.

St Paul's, Deptford is a beautiful old church built during the reign of Queen Anne in 1730. Described by former Poet Laureate Sir John Betjeman as 'the pearl in the heart of Deptford', it is built in the baroque style.

The church's interior contains some interesting memorials to seafarers. The Rev. Noel Mellish came to St Paul's as curate in 1912. During the First World War he was awarded the Victoria Cross, Britain's highest medal for bravery, for rescuing 22 men while under heavy machine-gun fire.

Of course, there are now many other churches in Lewisham of all different denominations. The old parishes of St Mary's, St Margaret's and St Paul's were divided into smaller parishes when new churches were built to serve the borough's rapidly growing population.

Many Lewisham churches were damaged or destroyed during the Second World War. Some have been pulled down or converted to other uses. Fewer churches are needed now: the number of people attending on a Sunday has fallen and those that do often prefer to worship in schools and other more informal settings.

LEE

William the Conqueror seized the manor of Lee from its Saxon tenant and gave it to Odo, Bishop of Bayeux. It was Odo who commissioned the famous Bayeux tapestry, which tells the story of William's victory over King Harold. At the time of the Domesday Book, about 70 people lived in Lee.

Much of the area was covered by woodland. Wood from the trees was burnt to make charcoal, which was sold in London. That's where the name 'Burnt Ash' comes from. By the 18th century, nearly all the trees had been cut down, to be replaced by fields.

Lee was largely a rural community, but between the 17th and 19th centuries several large houses were built in the village for wealthy City merchants. The Manor House and Pentland House in Old Road, and the Cedars in Belmont Hill, are the only ones left.

The Manor House was built in 1772. It was bought by Sir Francis Baring in 1796. Sir Francis was a very rich man who was a member of the well-known firm of merchant bankers, Baring Brothers. In 1899, the family sold the house to Lewisham Borough Council, who turned it into a library, while the grounds became a park.

Lee Place, another large house in Old Road, was the home of Christopher Boone, a rich merchant. In 1683, he gave a piece of land in Lee High Road to the Merchant Taylors Company for almshouses and a chapel. The almshouses were for six poor people and a school mistress, who taught 12 local children – the boys to read and the girls to knit and sew! When the Boone family estate was sold in 1824, the Merchant Taylors Company built their own almshouses, which are still in use today. Boone's almshouses were demolished in 1876 but the chapel is still there.

The fertile soil in Lee made it a great place for dairy farming, crop growing and market gardening, although the Quaggy, which was much deeper than it is now, was liable to flood.

There was a large village green at Lee Green, complete with stocks to punish petty criminals. The Tiger's Head Inn on the green attracted many customers with its prize fights, cricket matches and bowling tournaments.

Lee remained a rural community until the 19th century, when it changed beyond all recognition. Gradually the grand houses were sold and knocked down. Streets of smaller houses were built in their grounds. Lee station was opened in 1866 and the population grew rapidly. New churches, shops and schools were built. Today, there are many modern buildings in Lee, some of which were built to fill the gaps caused by bombing during the Second World War.

WHAT'S IN A NAME?

Lewisham place names can tell us a lot about the borough's history. Some are very ancient names associated with the earliest Anglo-Saxon settlers or features of the landscape that have long since vanished. Others appeared later as new settlements sprung up.

Bell Green: until the end of the 18th century Bell Green was called Sydenham Green and comes from the original Bell pub which stood on the northern edge of the green until about 1780.

Bellingham: the Old English word 'ham' can mean a settlement or village, or it can mean a meadow, especially a water meadow. The name Bellingham may come from the Beringas, a tribe who were early settlers in the area. Another possible meaning is 'the settlement of the dwellers at the hill'.

Blackheath: comes from the fact that the soil of the heath, or perhaps the bushes that covered it, were dark: black heath. It used to be spelt Blachehedfeld.

Brockley: comes from two Old English words, 'broc' (a brook) and 'leah' (a clearing or glade). It means a clearing in the marsh. Another possible meaning is 'the clearing where Broca lives'. Sometimes it was spelt Brocele and Brockele.

Catford: means 'the ford frequented by cats' (across the River Ravensbourne).

Deptford: comes from the Old English words meaning deep ford.

Downham: commemorates Lord Downham, Chairman of the London County Council. Interestingly, the Old English meaning of his name is 'the settlement on a hill'.

Forest Hill: in the Middle Ages the area was known as 'The Forest' and was used in the 1790s by the developer of Honor Oak Road, the original Forest Hill.

Grove Park: probably named after a farm that was situated there called Grove Farm.

Hatcham: appears to come from a personal name and means 'the settlement of Haecci'. It used to be spelt Hacchesham.

Hither Green: in the early 19th century the lower part of Hither Green Lane was known as Further Green. So it seems that Hither Green may have meant 'the nearer green'.

Honor Oak: after Queen Elizabeth I dined under an oak tree at this spot it was known from then on as the Oak of Honour. It sometimes appears on maps as Oak of Arnon, which may just indicate how people used to pronounce it.

Ladywell: comes from a well which used to be there, known as the Lady or Lady's Well. It is almost certainly connected to Lewisham's church, which is dedicated to St Mary the Virgin (Our Lady).

Lee: comes from the Old English word 'leah' meaning a wood or a clearing in a wood.

Lewisham: comes from the Old English words 'Leofe's, or Leofsa's, ham', meaning 'the settlement or village of Leof'. We don't know who Leof was, but he probably lived in the sixth century.

New Cross: the district takes its name from an inn originally called the Golden Cross, which changed its name to New Cross House.

Rushey Green: named after the rushes that used to grow alongside the marshy green.

Southend: self-explanatory: the village of Southend lay at the southern end of the parish of Lewisham!

Sydenham: means 'the village or settlement of Sipa (or Cippa)'. Other early spellings include Cyppenham, Sipeham, Syppenham and Sidenham. One theory is that Sipa was a nickname for a drunkard.

▼ Lewisham High Street in the 1870s... now the location of the shopping centre

LEWISHAM

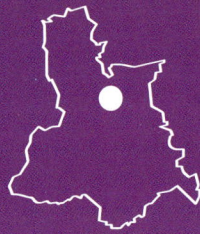

The Domesday Book tell us that the manor of Lewisham was home to a large farming community, with 11 watermills and 300 people.

The Abbot of St Peter's in Ghent was the Lord of the Manor but, being located in Belgium, he would have appointed a resident Prior to act on his behalf. The Prior lived in the middle of Lewisham in a manor house with a chapel, surrounded by farm buildings and, possibly, a moat. The Lewisham Priory is thought to have been located near St Mary's parish church.

The Lord of the Manor was entitled to payments and tolls from his tenants, including fees for grinding corn in one of the manor's watermills, port charges, fines for allowing animals to stray on the road and charges when land was inherited. Tenants were also expected to help bring in the harvest, supplying both labour and equipment. In return, they were given their own strips of land to cultivate and rights to graze animals on the common land.

The main crops grown in Lewisham were wheat and barley. Following the Black Death, which swept the country in the early 14th century, killing over one-third of the population, sheep farming became the norm, as it required less manpower.

By the 17th century, Lewisham had developed into a village. At its heart was the parish church, St Mary's, around which were clustered a few cottages, with houses starting to be built along the main roads.

The High Street was lined with elm trees and had a stream running through it. Lewisham was a very picturesque, rural village, quite different from the bustling town centre we see today! In time, larger houses and villas started to appear along the High Street for the wealthier families, who were attracted by the town's rural charm and its proximity to the City of London.

The 19th century was a period of great change for the town. Until then, Lewisham was still an agricultural community, its residents mostly earning a living from farming, market gardening, milling and brick-making. The coming of the railways made it possible for workers to live in 'Leafy Lewisham' and commute to jobs in the City every day.

Farms and many of the grand houses gradually started to disappear to make way for row after row of small houses. By the end of the century, Lewisham had lost its rural character altogether. The population increased dramatically, doubling between 1881 and 1901.

Although Lewisham had lost many of its wealthier residents and gained many poor ones, the town was still remarkably prosperous. A survey taken at the time indicated that Lewisham had a lower percentage of poor residents, and a higher percentage of well-off ones, than Kensington and Chelsea!

Around the start of the 20th century, industry began to return to the town and new shops were built to serve the new residents. Some smaller shops were combined to create department stores, the most famous of which was Chiesmans, which later became the Army and Navy. The Police station now occupies its site.

The Clock Tower was built to commemorate Queen Victoria's Diamond Jubilee in 1897, the 60th year of her reign. It was funded by public donations but failed to reach its target, so is missing the planned panels on the side featuring the borough's coats-of-arms.

Many buildings in the High Street were damaged in Second World War bombing raids and were eventually replaced with chain stores and larger shops. In 1955, the 7,500 sq ft Sainsbury's at Lewisham was considered the largest supermarket in Europe. The Riverdale Shopping Centre opened in 1977; it was renamed 'Lewisham shopping' in 2007. Most of Lewisham's old buildings have disappeared, but if you look carefully you may spot some older houses lurking behind the modern shop fronts.

▶ Architect's drawing of the Lewisham Clocktower

ALIEN ABBOTS

The first recorded mention of Lewisham was in a royal charter of 964, when King Edgar gave the manor, which included Greenwich, Woolwich, Mottingham and Coombe, to the Abbey of St Peter at Ghent, in Belgium. It was a reward for sheltering the then exiled Abbot Dunstan, a good friend and supporter of the king. Dunstan later became Archbishop of Canterbury and, on his death, one of Britain most's popular saints.

Another charter suggests that the gift of Lewisham lands was made 46 years earlier by Elstrudis, the youngest daughter of King Alfred the Great. However, this charter has since proved to be a forgery, and not a very good one at that. It was not unusual in the Middle Ages to produce counterfeit documents in order to prove land ownership rights!

Over the next 500 years, those rights to the manor of Lewisham were hotly contested. The Abbot of St Peter's lost them several times, then gained them back, and had to seek confirmation from every new king. In 1295, with a threat of invasion from the French, all foreigners were viewed as potential spies, including monks! 'Alien' or foreign religious orders came under suspicion and were seen as a rich source of income for the king, so once again the Abbot lost control of the manor. Finally, after years of wrangling and mounting debts, and continuing fears that alien priories were diverting money to fund the King of France's war effort, the manor was returned to Royal ownership in 1414.

The manors of Lewisham and Greenwich, including all their land and income, were subsequently given by King Henry V to one of three new monasteries he had built: Charterhouse of Jesus of Bethlehem at Shene (now Richmond).

But it was not to stay with the new monastery for very long. King Henry VIII found his existing palace at Greenwich a little too cramped and took a liking to the nearby farmland now owned by the Prior of Shene. Henry 'persuaded' the prior to part with the manor in exchange for land in Buckinghamshire and elsewhere.

In the end, it made little difference. Like his predecessors, Henry wanted to reduce the Church's power in England, as well as raise money to finance his expensive wars against France and Scotland. Finally, when the Pope refused to grant him a divorce from Catherine of Aragon, Henry retaliated by establishing his own church – the Church of England – declaring himself its Supreme Head. In 1536, Henry ordered the closing down of all the abbeys, monasteries and convents across England, Wales and Ireland. This 'Dissolution' took four years to complete. Henry had set off a process in this country known as the Reformation, when England stopped being a Roman Catholic country and became Protestant. And where did all the money go? Into the coffers of the king and his cronies!

NEW CROSS & HATCHAM

New Cross may have got its name from an old inn called the New Cross House. Stone House in Lewisham Way is now one of the oldest houses in the area. It was built between 1766 and 1774 and was known as the Comical House, because of its strange shape! Goldsmiths College nearby was originally the Royal Naval School. It opened in 1843 and was where the sons of 'naval and military officers in needy circumstances' were educated.

Running through New Cross is the London to Dover road. This Roman road was also the route taken by pilgrims travelling to

St Thomas Becket's tomb at Canterbury, made famous in Geoffrey Chaucer's *Canterbury Tales*.

The Manor of Hatcham, near New Cross, was a tiny village until the 18th century, when market gardens started to spring up to provide fresh fruit and vegetables for the people of London.

In 1795, an Admiralty semaphore station was built on the top of Plow Garlic Hill, later renamed Telegraph Hill. This was used to relay messages before the electric telegraph was invented. The news of the Duke of Wellington's victory over Napoleon at the Battle of Waterloo was passed on to London via the Hatcham semaphore station.

The village was a pleasant and convenient place for wealthy people to live. One of these was Joseph Hardcastle, who owned a large mansion called Hatcham House. Joseph was a member of an influential group of people called the Clapham Sect, who fought for the abolition of the slave trade. They would often meet at Hatcham House to plan their opposition.

The slopes of Telegraph Hill were developed by the Haberdasher's Company, with wide tree-lined streets and large houses. In 1875, the Company also built boys and girls secondary schools, named after Robert Aske, a former Master of the Company, who left money in 1690 for a school and almshouse.

◀ The Admiralty semaphore station on what became known as Telegraph Hill

SCHOOL'S OUT!

Before an Act of Parliament of 1870 made attendance at elementary school compulsory, many children went without a proper education.

Early schools were often run by charities or churches. One of Lewisham's earliest and best-known schools is Colfe's Grammar School, which was established in Lewisham by the local vicar, Rev. Abraham Colfe, in 1652. It was a fee-paying school for boys, but '31 sons of poor men' were also admitted on scholarships. The standard of education was high and older boys were expected to speak to each other and to the teachers in Latin!

There were a number of schools in the borough for children of wealthy parents. Poor children, if they had any education at all, often attended 'dame' schools. These were usually run by a woman who gave a basic education to local children in her own home.

From the 18th century onwards, charity schools were founded to give poorer children an education. A good example was John Addey's School. Addey was a Deptford shipbuilder who died in 1606, leaving £200 in his will for the poor of the town. It was discovered in 1820 that the money had never been been used properly and so a school was built in his name in Church

◀ A Victorian school boy in around 1880

Street in 1822. About 200 local children were educated there, mainly from large families with small incomes. Pupils who behaved well were allowed to wear a school uniform: a brown suit for the boys and brown dresses with white caps and aprons for the girls. In 1893 Addey's School joined with another charity school, Dr Stanhope's, which was opened in 1723. The present Addey and Stanhope School was built in New Cross Road in 1900.

The Church of England began to build its own schools from 1811 onwards. Known as National Schools, they offered primary education to all children. In Lee, for example, the National School in Church Street was opened in 1839. Before this time most of Lee's poor children were employed by local farmers and received schooling only on Sundays.

The Deptford Ragged School opened in 1844. It was called that because the children who attended were dressed in rags and went around in bare feet in all weathers. The school was founded by William Agutter, a member of the Deptford Congregational Church, who was appalled at the wretched conditions the children lived in. Agutter and his friends rented a room in what is now Addey Street and crammed in as many children as possible on Sundays, teaching them Bible stories and how to read and write. The school grew and grew and thousands of Deptford children would attend every week, day or night.

Many of Lewisham's best-known schools date from the 19th century: Haberdasher Aske's Schools at Hatcham; Blackheath High School for Girls; St Dunstan's College, Catford; and Prendergast School, Rushey Green (now on Hilly Fields).

The Blackheath Proprietary School in Blackheath Village, which existed between 1831 and 1908, adopted a very unusual approach. It was run like a business; parents bought shares in the school, which entitled them to send their children there. The Proprietary School was very successful, with former pupils becoming judges, MPs, lawyers, civil servants, soldiers, as well as excellent athletes.

▶ Dr Williams' private school in Deptford, probably around the 1860s

SOUTHEND, DOWNHAM & BELLINGHAM

Southend was the last part of the borough of Lewisham to become built up. There were two watermills on the River Ravensbourne there, called the Upper and Lower Mills. The river was much deeper then, so there was plenty of water to turn the mills' waterwheels.

In the early 18th century, the Lower Mill belonged to the How family, who were famous for manufacturing high quality cutlery. It later became a mustard mill, then a corn mill. In the late 19th century the Upper Mill belonged to Jacob Perry, who used it to generate electricity, cut wood and prepare cattle feed. Perry was clearly a man of many talents: he also made cricket bats from the willow trees that grew on his farm!

During the 19th century, the village of Southend was dominated by the Forster family, who owned a lot of the land. They lived at Southend Hall near the junction of Whitefoot Lane and Bromley Road. Sadly, Lord Forster's two sons were killed in the First World War. In 1919, his Lordship gave part of his estate to Lewisham Council and Forster Memorial Park was created in memory of his sons.

In the late 19th century, Southend was still a peaceful little village, with fruit and vegetable wagons trundling through on their way from Kent to London. A village school was opened in 1855. Pupils paid one penny a week for their education and were given a pair of hobnail boots at Christmas!

Rail travel came to Southend in 1892, when the Nunhead to Shortlands railway was opened. At the outbreak of the First World War in 1914, the village was still surrounded by fields, allotments and sports grounds. During the 1920s and 1930s, new streets of houses turned Southend into another London suburb.

Beckenham Place Park is the largest green space in the borough and was opened to the public in 1929. Beckenham Place mansion and the surrounding grounds were once home to the timber merchant John Cator, who had bought the rights to the manor of Beckenham in 1773. The grand building's front entrance or 'portico' was rescued from Wricklemarsh House in Blackheath before it was broken up. During the Second World

◄ Some manufacturers were so jealous of the success of *How* cutlery that they stamped the name *Now* onto theirs to try and fool buyers!

War, Beckenham Place Park was used as a Prisoner of War camp and as a site for anti-aircraft guns and barrage balloons.

Bellingham housing estate was built by the London County Council shortly after the First World War. It provided much needed work for local building labourers, contractors and suppliers. The Bellingham site was previously farmland. Around 2,670 houses and flats were built.

Downham was also open countryside until the 1920s. The London County Council decided to buy two local farms, Holloway and Shroffold, and between 1924 and 1930 built a huge housing estate. The name Downham only came into being when the estate was built, after the Chairman of the London County Council at the time, Lord Downham.

Over 6,000 new homes were built. Many of the people who moved there were from East London slums. A number of streets on the Downham estate are named after characters from the legend of King Arthur, including Launcelot, Geraint and Galahad... and no-one really knows why.

An early resident of the Downham estate was Richard Harrow, one of the world's heaviest men. When he died in 1936, he weighed over 40 stone; his chest measured 6ft, his waist 6ft and his collar 26 inches!

▶ Harvesting at Springhill Farm, later to become the site of the Downham estate

THE GREAT GLASSHOUSE

The Crystal Palace was built in Hyde Park in London in 1851 to house the Great Exhibition. It was the brainchild of a group of prominent Victorians, headed by Queen Victoria's husband, Prince Albert. Countries all over the world sent examples of their art, crafts and industrial goods to be displayed.

The Crystal Palace was designed by Joseph Paxton, who began his career as a gardener's assistant. He must have been a very good gardener, as the Duke of Devonshire offered him the job of Head Gardener at his grand house at Chatsworth in Derbyshire, when Paxton was just 22. Paxton built several greenhouses at Chatsworth and, when he heard that a huge building was needed for the Great Exhibition, he drew up plans for the biggest greenhouse in the world!

Even though the Crystal Palace was a big building, it only took nine months to build. It was three times longer than St Paul's Cathedral and contained over 293,000 panes of glass and 24 miles of gutters.

The Exhibition was a great success. It was open for less than five months, but over six million people came to see the exhibits, many of which were very strange! They included a penknife with 1,851 blades, a collapsible piano, a bed which tipped its occupant onto the floor at a certain time and a carriage pulled by kites. The Exhibition's centrepiece was an 8.2m high solid crystal fountain. Queen Victoria went to the Exhibition 40 times and one old lady of 85 walked all the way from Penzance in Cornwall to see it.

When the Exhibition closed, no-one was quite sure what to do with the Crystal Palace. Eventually, Joseph Paxton formed a company which bought the building, along with some land just outside the borough in Sydenham. There he could rebuild it, bigger and better than the original. The Sydenham building was actually 50% larger than the one at Hyde Park. Its grounds were just as impressive, with lawns, flower beds, lakes, models of prehistoric monsters and stunning fountains.

▼ The spectacular Egyptian Court, complete with sphinxes and giant statues

▶ The magnificent Crystal Palace and pleasure gardens attracted millions of visitors

The new Exhibition was due to be opened by Queen Victoria in June 1854, but earlier in that year a letter arrived from '13 eminent persons', expressing a concern that the naked male statues might offend Victorian decency. With the threat of a nationwide protest campaign, and under pressure to open the Exhibition in time, the offending items were removed with a hammer and chisel... and covered with a plaster fig leaf!

The new building featured a series of rooms displaying the art and architecture from different historical periods. There was also a large concert hall with space for 4,000 musicians and singers. Spectacular firework displays were held regularly in the grounds.

The new Crystal Palace was a great success and around two million people visited it every year. But it never made much profit and the building needed constant repairs and repainting to prevent it looking shabby.

Disaster struck on the night of 30 November 1936, when the Crystal Palace was destroyed by fire. The glow of the flames could be seen right across London. It was never rebuilt and the grounds are now a park and home to the National Recreation Centre.

You can still see the remains of some of the terraces, where a giant stone head of Joseph Paxton now gazes out across the sad remains of his architectural masterpiece.

▶ 30 November 1936: fire fighters battle in vain to save the Crystal Palace

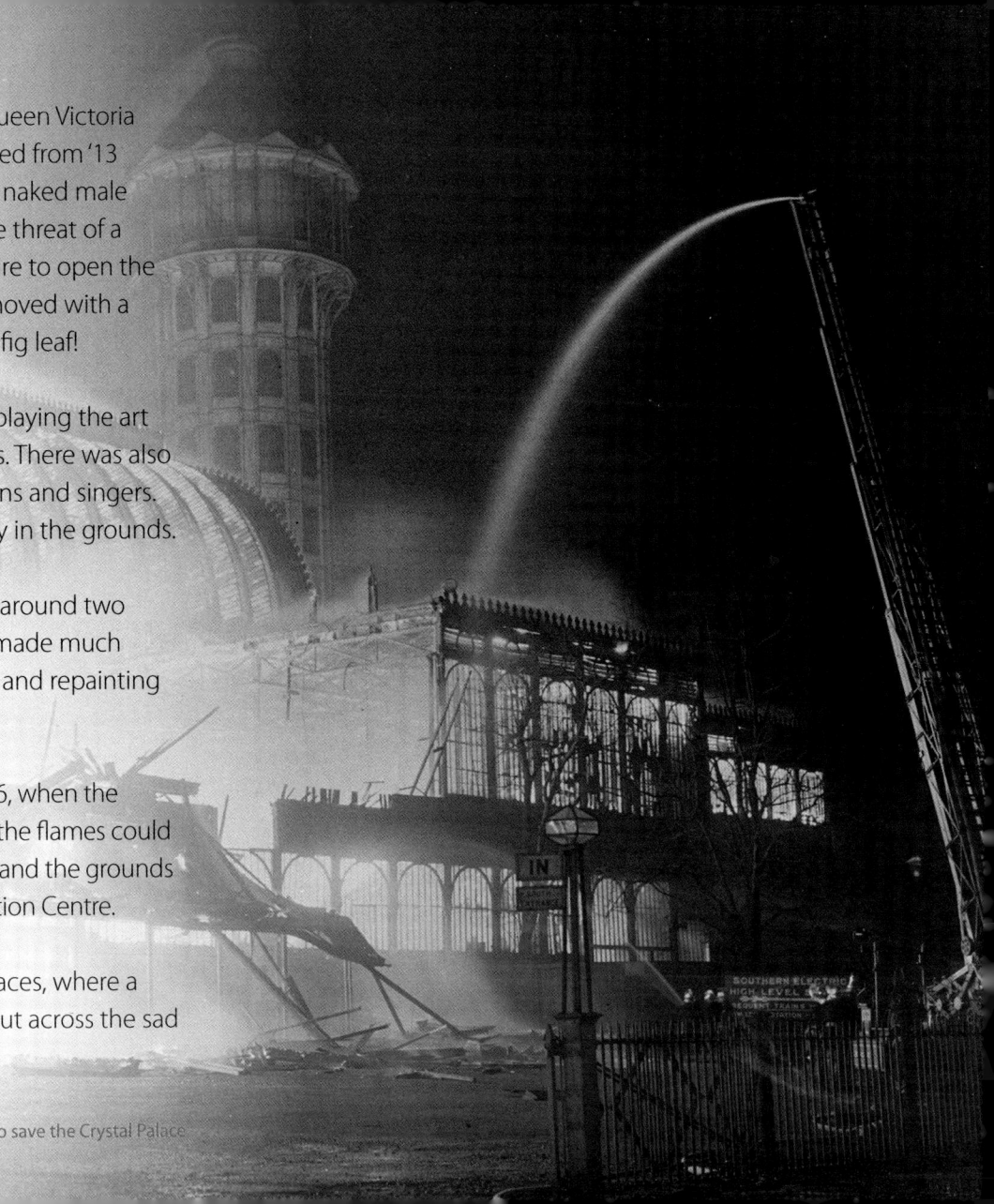

SYDENHAM

In the Middle Ages, Sydenham was a wild, isolated area, mostly covered by Westwood Forest. There were a few cottages along what is now Sydenham Road, surrounded by orchards and market gardens, with farm fields beyond.

Place House, the Manor House of Sydenham, was once home to Dr William Aubrey, a judge and friend of Elizabeth I. The Queen often consulted William, whom she called 'her little doctor', and visited him at Place House. The mansion was located near the junction of Catford Hill and Perry Hill. Bell Green is said to get its name from a bell tower built on the Place House estate to warn of approaching visitors. However, it is more likely to be named after the Bell pub that stood on the site.

Westwood Forest was gradually cut down from the 16th century onwards, mainly to provide timber for the Deptford shipyards. Local people grazed their sheep and cattle on what became Westwood Common, a right that had existed for centuries. However, in 1614, three courtiers tried to grab the common land for themselves. They put up fences to prevent the villagers from using it. The vicar of Lewisham, Rev. Abraham Colfe, led 500 people on a protest march to London, where they presented a petition to the king. The case went to court and the villagers finally won back the right to use the common. However, an Act of Parliament in 1810 led to all common land being enclosed and Westwood Common was gradually built over.

In the mid-17th century springs of 'medicinal' water were discovered at Sydenham, where Wells Park is now situated. Crowds of people would come on Sundays to 'take the waters', including King George III, who used to stay at a little cottage there. The wells were popular until the early 19th century, when they went out of fashion.

A fascinating railway experiment took place in the town in the 1840s. Called the atmospheric railway, it made use of trains driven

▶ Place House in 1791

solely by vacuum pressure. A special line was built through Forest Hill, Sydenham and Croydon for the revolutionary trains, which ran between 1845 and 1847. They were quiet and clean, but very unreliable because rats kept eating the leather flaps that helped create the vacuum, and so this pioneering green transport scheme had to be scrapped!

Many new houses were built in Sydenham during the 19th century. Although the Crystal Palace itself was located just outside of the borough, it had a huge impact on housing development in Sydenham.

Upper Sydenham was a smart area, where well-off people built large houses on the high ground. A number of these houses were occupied by senior officials and directors of the Crystal Palace Company. Smaller, poorer housing was built down in Lower Sydenham. Some of these houses were originally intended for the workers at the Crystal Palace Gas Company, which was built on the banks of the River Pool at Bell Green in 1858.

After 1854, when the Crystal Palace moved to Sydenham, the town became a very fashionable place in which to live. Several famous people of their time had homes there, including the Antarctic explorer Sir Ernest Shackleton, whose family lived at Westwood Hill, and the famous cricketer, Dr W G Grace, who lived at Lawrie Park Road.

▶ Ernest Shackleton aged 16